REACH FOR THE LIGHT

Easter
"Poetik Desire"
Dodds

Even while navigating the darkest of life's tunnels...
perseverance, hope, and faith
shall lead you to the light at the end of that tunnel!

Wider Perspectives Publishing   ¤ 2025 ¤   Hampton Roads, Va.

© 2025, Easter Dodds, including writing as *Poetik Desire*
1st run complete in August 2025 Wider Perspectives Publishing, Hampton Roads, Va.
ISBN 978-1-964531-40-3

Dedication

To all the dreamers hesitant to break through fear and doubt:

Climb that mountain
Harboring a valley of dreams
For once you dare reach its peak
Discover a view of endless possibilities
The world is within your reach
Make your mark
Spread love
Inspire!

Prelude: Journey Beyond the Flame to Self-Discovery

Like a moth to the flame
Don't get burned by the fire
Where your attraction to its flickering glow
Is ignited by forces unseen, unknown
Luring you in to elusive desires
You are not yet ready to acquire

Instead, be the crawling caterpillar
Taking its time to discover its life's path
Drawn to embrace the shadows of a cocoon
To welcome the darkness of transformation
Blossoming into your true self
Through meditative mentalities attuned

Let your curiosity be the spark
To set ablaze your dreamt freedoms
Where you have become a butterfly
Captivated by the light of emerging promises
Soaring into enlightened rays of shining possibilities
Ready for every new beginning to explore its kingdoms

Introduction

We all strive for a better way of life as we seek ways to break through our darkest shadows and into the light. We live our lives unsure of the direction life's road will take us. With uncertainty, our paths lead us through many journeys in hopes that we may find our true destiny. What is your destined career? What is your destined love affair? What has been predestined for your life – the reason for your birth?

Through all its twists and turns, the roadmap of life will travel through days of joy and nights of sorrow. Relationships you form will become sweet and then sour along an endless search for your true love. Your career goals are expected to change as you search for that "dream job". Through any search for whatever is your passion or dream, despairs of financial struggles and emotional turmoil will always be found nearby.

You must learn to believe, to hope, to have faith despite all your fears as you blindly travel on your journeys through life. For through all of life's uncertain storms casting gloomy reflections upon your journeys, it's inevitable that rainbow clouds will soon appear; as through those clouds will be seen rays of light shining towards your destined path.

Come and take a journey through a selection of poetry exploring the joys and struggles we face in chasing after our dreams and our destinies, where our darkest despairs are soon left behind as we reach for the light.

Enlightened Seeker
[*Haiku*]

Peeking through branches
Looking amidst the treetops
Searching for sunlight

Reach for the Light

These walls are closing in on me
Blinded by darkness, I walk forward aimlessly
Through a long, dark tunnel groping my way
Towards a light I seek of brighter days

I'm trapped in a place where there's no going back
Bittered by truth that what once was, now resides in the past
The future I'm unable to foresee now hangs in the balance
Like that of this tunnel I travel through life's next challenge

While navigating the darkest of life's tunnels
I'll try not to let myself become too fearful
Of a fate that has always been out of my control
Wherever my story leads next, God has planned the road

I must trust in the life I've been given to live
Trust in the challenges that shall hold me captive
As I learn to search and reach for the light
That breaks me free, out of my darkest plight

Where perseverance, hope, and faith
Shall prove that anything good, is worth the wait
For this is all you need to reach for that light
Shining brightly at the end, where you and destiny unite

Contents

I Chasing Dreams

II Like a Caged Bird

VI   Painted Destiny

VII   At the Kiss of Twilight

Explore Poetic Forms
Meet Your Poet

Chasing Dreams

"Hold fast to dreams, for if dreams die,
life is a broken-winged bird that cannot fly"

- Langston Hughes

| : | Roadmap of Life | : |

The roadmap of life swerves
Through many twists and turns

Filled with different obstacles
Of life lessons learned

Where the path driven rarely
Runs straight and narrow

As happy, easy travels
Filled with little sorrow

More often we must steer through
Unforeseen rough bumps up ahead

Yield to speeding temptations of fear
Learn maneuvers to strengthen your life's tread

The potholes of worn-out excursions
We sink and dip into along the way

Represent where lasting impressions
Of similar forked journeys have been made

It's like our friends and family
Whom we share with in this adventure

Leaving lasting impressions in our life
Their love and support propel us forward

Because the roadmap of life
A long journey indeed

Is filled with many changes
Affecting the life we lead

These changes we face
And how we navigate through them

Is what shapes who we'll be
In the winding roads ahead

Be a Chameleon, Change Your Colors

Life is all about change and adaptations

Change your colors...

Adapt to your surroundings...

Blend well and be camouflaged

In the obstacles that come your way

*[*Title is a Six-Word Memoir]*

Obstacles

Obstacles block
Your way in life

        With challenges you face
        Day after day

                Trying to set
                Just the right pace

    To break through these obstacles
    Standing in your way

                It's easy to say
                I'll get through today

But harder to believe
You'll overcome the shadows

        To step out of disparity
        In attempts to solve your problems

                'Til you see the light of day
                Seeking a joyous rise from sorrow

    It's inevitable that one day soon
    You'll jump clear through

            All of these obstacles
            That have come to face you

Poetik Desire

With no problems or worries
But beware
                              'Cause soon enough
                         Those obstacles will stare you…

                                        Straight in the face
                                     To hinder your travels

          Becoming yet another day
          Full of worried sorrow

                              Ensuring you're never complacent
                                With the life you're here to live

Obstacles arrive in a hurry
Keeping your life in limbo

Uncertainty of Life

Life's journey follows a path
Along the road of uncertainty

Arriving
at
all
r
o   k
f   s

in   the   road

Where life's t w i s t s and t u r n s shall meet

For at every turn life's journey makes
A decision, a choice must be made

To choose to go "left" - - - -   OR - - - -   choose to go "right"

Not knowing if our decision has a price to be paid

For all our choices, good and bad
Has its consequences and/or rewards

But you must always trust what's in your heart
And choose wisely as you move on forward

Just believe in yourself and in God
Because everything happens for a reason

                              Even the struggles that we must face
                                    Will only last for a season

                  Though the uncertainty of life

Can bring you joy or fear
                              Which way on your journey

                  Through life will you steer?

Forked Bends...

Either forked bend sways different extremes.

[Six-Word Memoir]

Face Hardships...

Face hardships. Overcome struggles. Become stronger.

[Six-Word Memoir]

Life Ain't Easy

Life ain't easy
It forever remains complicated

Too many decisions   Too many choices   Too many struggles

to climb   o
obstacles   v
many   e
Too   r

I'm going   O U T of my mind
I've just gone c R a Z y
I don't know what to do anymore
I don't know what's happening to me

I've got a love life that's all ScReWeD up
Just can't seem to find Mr. Right

Yet I've got a wonderful life set out for me
When it comes to college/career life

I've got everything going for me
So why do I feel so alone

Why do these tears keep flowing
Through this pool of uncertainty

All I want is to be happy
    Free-spirited and carefree

        All I want is to find Mr. Right
            Someone who'll always be there for me

                But life ain't easy
            It forever remains complicated

        Have I made the right decisions
    We'll just have to wait and see

Spice of Life...

Spice of life: Opportunities changing possibilities.

[Six-Word Memoir]

Better Tomorrows...

Todays are yesterdays becoming better tomorrows.

[Six-Word Memoir]

Change Often Occurs Without Your Permission

Life travels a steady pace
>>> Expected routines
>>> Expected outcomes
>>> Expected days of "normalcy"
>>>>> Not expecting concerns
>>>>> To deal with any worries
Things appear to be A-OK
>>> No cloudy skies of gray linger
>>> Nothing foreshadows
>>> Threatening blows
>>>>> To happiness becoming despair

So when things seem "perfect"
>>> Like the ending of a Hallmark movie
>>> When everything seems to fall into place

Step back for a moment
>>> And realize that soon
>>> Something big or small
>>> Is bound to happen
>>>>> To affect your current pace
>>>>> And cause... an unwelcomed change

We all know life is never easy
>>> When it does become easy
>>> You still can't let your guard down

Because whether you feel
You may have control over your choices
                    Control over your life
                    Control over what will happen
                    Control over what you want, need, or desire

That sense of control
                    Can easily be swept away from you
                    Like a Houdini trick
                    Like the rug being pulled out from under you

As you strive to land back in place
                            Yet, instead may feel
                            You're about to fall flat on your face

For that is what life does best...
                    Playing tricks on you
                            Throwing you those fast curve balls

To see how well you think on your feet
To see how well you fall and get back up
To see how well a challenge can grow you
To see how well your fears can turn into strength

This change can often happen in an instant
                            Without your permission
                            Without forewarning
                            Without hesitation

That change begs of you
        To think about something old
        Now becoming, adapting, and transitioning
        Into something new

Your old way of life will no longer be the same
You must rummage through it like a day of spring cleaning

What old habits
        Old ways of thinking
        Old routines and expectations
                Should you now get rid of
                For something even better?

A new way of thinking is very refreshing
It can re-spark fiery embers of inspired thinking
        As you contemplate new journeys
        New experiences to enjoy

A new habit can bring about a better you
        Uplifting your self-confidence
        Encouraging you to be brave
        Pushing you to live healthier
        Inspiring you to provide better self-care

This change may soon force you to see
        What you didn't know you had to get rid of
        In order to welcome something more qualitative

Change can occur without permission
        So when it does
        Grab the reigns and hold on tight

The ride will get a bit bumpy
        Full of twists and turns
        Forks in the road
        Forcing hard decisions
        But you will find your way again
Slowly and carefully
        Take deep breaths
        Analyze your life's choices
        Discover a new path to follow
Granting permission
        To forge your way through
        To the next brighter day

To accept the hidden reason
        Why this change has happened
        Why life has shifted
        And forced you to alter its course

*[*Title is a Six-Word Memoir]*

The Dawn of Adulthood

There comes a time in one's life
A time for transformative change
When one will grow up and adapt
To a lifestyle rearranged

Years of innocence have flown by
The era of maturity ventures on
Variations of life's comforts and stability
Evolves into a rising new dawn

Childhood is left behind
When encroaching adulthood begins
New fears and experiences
Rapidly come pouring in

Too quickly comes the time
When one must spread their wings
To explore their own independence
Without parental guidance interfering

A new foundation is self-built
Upon stacked blocks of responsibilities
Formation of this journeyed existence
Reaches far beyond a world of possibilities

Possibilities for a destined career
Hopefully leading to desired prosperity
Possibilities for true love and marriage
Molding your own rulebook for raising a family

Poetik Desire

There inevitably comes a time in one's life
A time for expected change
When one will grow up and evolve
Into a life your choices arranged

Embrace Evolution of Self

Dare to be challenged
Step out of your comfort zone
Experience growth

[Haiku]

Challenges Dared...

Challenges dared. New you. Growth experienced.

[Six-Word Memoir]

The Power of Perspective

All it TAKES is just...

A little more *FOCUS*

A little more WORK

```
        t    of   t
        u         h
STEP  o        e  BOX
```

tWeAk your qUiRkS

OPEN your *mind*

OLD habits be *banished*

eVoLvE your *perspective*

Be SURPRISED what's *accomplished*!

Rules Define...

Rules define expectations; rise to occasion.

[Six-Word Memoir]

Rules Are There for a Reason!
[Couplet Verses]

Rules are there for a reason
Though not set in stone, they can be "broken"

Still… rules are there so that one may adhere
To a certain code or standard

No one likes change, no one likes "structure"
We all desire "freedom of speech"

All that is demanded of you is to respect
What is desired to be expected of you

Respect that someone wants you to strive
To adhere to a higher standard, to evolve… to grow…

For without growth and evolution
We would still be the former primates of our own selves

Never learning to be the best of what we could be
In anything in this life that we live

Rules are there for a reason
Follow the rules or decide to bend and break them

Either way, playing by the rules or avoiding them entirely
Hurts not only you but those around you too

Handlebars of Life
[Couplet Verses]

Visualize, conceptualize, hands outreached
Fingers, secured, tightly leeched

Invisible, indiscernible, abstract concept
Life, a bike, handlebars nonexistent

Gripping, clasping, at thin air
Needing, security, in life's affairs

Balance, sustained, wheeling courses
Through, issues, of life's voyages

Handlebars, the starred, feature of life
Catcher, supporter, safety net of life

Feeling, anticipating, wobbling sensation
Needing, to swerve, avoid "plummetation"

Peddling, proceeding, through life's obstacles
Never, hinder, to seek trails of detours

Searching, reaching, gripping onto sanity
Searching, reaching, when lost in uncertainty

Searching, reaching, feeling security
Progressively, proceeding, gripped to life's necessity

A game, played, one called life
Ready, for activities, that are child-like

Safely, playing, rules adhered
Listening, to rattling, of mother's forefinger

Implying, a thinking, cautious wisdom
Scolds, behold, her overprotective anthem

When we've, dared be, ever so dangerous
Provoke, broke, life's golden promises

A prime, time, example exposed
Child, defying, what Mother's proposed

Seeking, sneaking, a moment of exhilaration
Is bold, evades scolds, resounds in exclamation

The hook: "Look! Look Ma, No Hands!"
Unafraid, brave: "Look Ma, No Hands!"

Tossing, excluding, defiance to rules
Capable, susceptible, to steadfast travels

Maintained, wheels untrained, fingers tightly gripped
Aimless mind, wanders blind, handlebars equipped

Unfocused, we've peddled, through life carefree
Gripping, clasping, onto life's necessity

Easily, daydreaming, of hopes and aspirations
Hoping, believing, in our life's visions

Unafraid, crusade, never fearing failure
Handled life, bars strife, protects its stumblers

Catcher, supporter, safety net of life
Why fear? Why appear? A coward of life

If always, bikeways, provide such security
Why be, so daring, to strip away assurities?

If, a whiff, of exhilaration is sought
Find, behind, is left daydreams to rot

Releasing, dependency, on handlebars of life
Allows, vows, of growth to ignite

Child, once smiled, played life carefree
Learning, not maturing, gripped to a guarantee

Adult, now consults, with mind of intrigue
Let loose, without excuse, defiance to proceed

In seeking, sneaking, moments of exhilaration
Questions, challenges, shouts in exclamation

The hook: "Look! Look Ma, No Hands!"
Unafraid, brave: "Look Ma, No Hands!"

Focused, determined, no longer just a dreamer
Focused, determined, a realist achiever

Focused, determined, taking a risk
Faster, faster, life is soon frisked

Unprotected, impacted, grip now loosens
Handlebars, fading far, into non-existence

Fearless, sprightliness, arms begin to extend
Conjecture: failure, lurks round the bend

Endangers, maneuvers, steering courses
Hands, command, fear not any bruises

Dangerous, action, calls for proclamation
Hands free, screaming banshee, shouts in exclamation

The hook: "Look! Look Ma, No Hands!"
Unafraid, brave: "Look Ma, No Hands!"

Frolicker, trickster, dares worldly adventures
Freewheeling, dreamings, life fully captured

Careless, success: "Look Ma, No Hands!"
Ultimate, balanced act: "Look Ma, No Hands!"

A Mindful Return

You'll get in return…
What your mind's thoughts shall allow
You to come to earn

[Haiku]

Bring to Fruition...

Bring to fruition your desires envisioned.

[Six-Word Memoir]

Speak Into Existence

What lies in your heart of desire
Requesting of you an existence acquired?

Close your eyes and wander
Your mind's abyss of darkness
Fondling through chambers
Of mystic details implicitly expressed
In thoughts arousing slumbering fantasies
Coursing through fibers of your being
Weaving webs of tangled tapestries
Where your heart of desire conceals
Coveted thoughts thoroughly enhancing
Every sensation you feel
As anxious anticipation awaits
Desire's discovered details
Preparing paths planned of surreal ideals
Endorsing engagements of existence

Speak into existence your heart's desires...
Along a journey fueled by yearning passion

Consuming your thoughts
Consuming your soul
Tantalizingly becoming
All you'll crave to know

Immerse yourself within hope's glimmering light
Shimmering in distant corners of your mind
As through your veins
Through synapses of your brain
Flows your desirable admirations

In rushing floods of inspiration
Through that dark abyss within
'Til a moment of realization
Sends lightning bolts of shocking revelations
Regurgitating up from
Deep dark pools of harbored thinkings
Soon spit out
From mouthed openings of spoken truths

Vomiting your heart's desire into its existence
A sickness of ambitious conjectures cured

Through proven expressions now overheard
Strewn out and about for others to take witness
Erect attention when voiced loud and clear
Spoken existence of what your heart begs all to hear
'Cause lusting after hopes and dreams
Bedded in self-reliant confinement
Surrenders its desired existence
To offers of assistance relinquished
Sealing all its secrets behind barred lips
Of desires entangled
In your mind's abyss of jailed silence
Seeking escape to freely flow
Waiting to hear you scream in echoes

Scream your intuitions
Scream your inhibitions
Scream your inspirations
Liberating isolated silence

Bring out from the dark
And into the light
Spoken truths and desires
Ready to take flight
Let the words roll off its landing strip
That is your tongue
'Til it reaches the tip
Pressed up against
The back door of your lips

Propelling your heart's desire
To force its way through
Breaking past surfaces of its
Imprisoned silence
Flying freely into winds
Of spoken existence
Gliding towards ears
Of those willing to listen, to hear
What it is you yearn for
And hold so dear

Open up your heart
Open up your mind
Open up your emotions
And be unguarded...

Be stripped like an open book
Spilling contents of your pages
Revealing vulnerabilities
Allowing your heart to be worn on sleeves
Of spoken susceptibilities
Where others may perceive
Ways to help you retrieve
What your heart of desire has conceived

Believe that what you speak
Lays between sheets of what your mind leaks
Impregnating a sneak peek glimpse
Into what your life seeks
Your thoughts evolve the emergence
Of your ripened states of reality
What you say and play on repeat
Is the looped track
You listen to subconsciously
Following habitually

Like rehearsed dance steps
Your views stepping in tune
Upon your trails influenced
By your state of mental cocoons

Guarding against imprinted portrayals
Of your karma spewed
Through thoughts spoken
Of how your life is viewed

Realizing how convergence
Of presumptuous virginal predispositions
Conjugates climatic ramblings
Of what our heart's desires
Soon birth of an existence

Don't let pools of subconscious speculations
Drown out attempts at disentanglements
Of your heart's desires fibrous aspects
Elaborately woven into tapestry garments
Awaiting cryptic clearance
To be deciphered and stripped
Where floods of inspiration shall flow and drip

Arousing revelations
Of ascertained introspection
Streaming through lips of diction
Your thoughts into creation

Poetik Desire

Downloaded and synced
The essence of lifestyles is linked
To karma's reflection
Of your speculated destinations
Where lustful cravings are soon acquired
Of your hopes, dreams, and desires
Salivating on the seductive art of temptation
That comes with speaking
What you wish into existence

Be not afraid to seek what you desire
Let not the journey be traveled at the expense
Of opportunities aloofly sequestered
To neglectful avoidance of needs for guidance
Learn to find yourself lying promiscuously in bed
With those who may help bring to fruition
What your heart and mind has lovingly envisioned
Brought about through your lips of desires
Spoken into existence

So tell me now... what lies in your heart of desire
Requesting of you an existence acquired?

Dreamer

confesse**D** reality desired

conjure**R** of wishes

mind's **E**ye sees

what it w**A**nts to believe

silent conte**M**plation

her dr**E**ams possess

extrao**R**dinary power

[Mesostics]

The Dreamworld Within
[Sestina]

Under twilight of
veiled eyes surrounded by
peace of tranquility, I
slowly reach into
my dreamworld where all
possibilities are mine to behold.

A wonderful place to behold
this getaway dreamscape of
escapism refuge for all
to feel liberated by
restraints of real world relinquished into
stress free paradise for you and I.

It's too surreal, I
feel it's all too real to behold
how lovely dreams morph into
fairy twinklings of
wishes I yearn to live by,
desiring truth granted to them all.

But when morning comes, sadly all
dreams do not get recalled by I
who sits upright in bed by
a window looking out to behold
my dreamworld of
paradise vanished, its realm cast into…

forgotten oblivion until into
the night once more comes all
my dearest wishes of
escapism returning back to I
who in sweet serenity does behold
sanctuaried residence to slumber by.

My dreamworld confined only by
subconscious mind slipping into
greater pipe dreams to behold
than what transpires in all
my waking hours, for I
imagine realities of

kingdoms to behold of fantasies floating by,
that which speaks of heart's desires into
glimpses of all dreamscapes, for the conjurer is I.

Dream Weaver
[Tanka Verses]

Stream of dreamless nights
Seeks to fill your sleepless mind
Under cover of
Swirling dreamy sights to spy
Lulling fantasies you'll find

Woven dreams released
As darkness begins to fall
Behind closed eyelids
Subconscious awakenings
Await beckoned call

Strings of images
Stitched together, bringing peace
A slumbering night
Resting restless subconscious
To awake refreshed

Revealing beauties
Of waking life's scenic trails
Dream Weaver, you are,
Tying dreamlike imageries
To each new day's unspun tale

Dreamcatcher

The crisp midnight air
Filled with dreams to declare
Within slumbering minds
Dreaming of destinies to find
An endless search
Begins atop a bedpost's perch
As I, the dreamcatcher,
Guides dreams through my inner circle

A circle created in unity and strength
Devised to give dreams ascent
To ride along my feathery wings
Into a dreamer's subconscious mainstream
These dreams become so crystal clear
Its dreamer shall have nothing to fear
For when the dreamer rises in the morn
A new reality for them has been adorned

Because I'm the dreamcatcher who rests
Upon slumbering dreams
Awakening you each day with
A captured dream, your new reality

As you slumber, never fear
I will never seek to steer
Unintended dreams your way
Only what is fated, passes my hallowed gateway
As within my surrounding tangled web
Is where unintended dreams are soon led
Trapped for a moment, 'til they are led astray
To seek its destined dreamer in the light of day

Fated dreams are well protected
By angels of dreams they are selected
Handled with care, such delicate packages
Are delivered into minds meant to receive its message
Demons of ambiguity
Trust the tangled webs within me
To capture unintended dreams
As to the rise of dawn, they are released to stream…

Through the crisp midnight air
Filled with dreams to declare
Within slumbering minds
Dreaming of destinies to find

What is Your Passion?

that which you can't walk away from
that which you seek no escape from
that which you turn to continually
that which you find salvation in
that which feeds your soul
that which feeds your mind
that which nourishes the passion you crave
that which your sanity it saves

[Anaphora]

The Veil of Dreams

in the darkness
hides the mystic unknown
where dreams desire
to seek lost worlds
of your life

[Free Form]

Finding Truth

Shut your eyes and ears
Tune out world, listen within
A truth is known, found

[Haiku]

Midnight Hour Murmurs Contemplative, Reflective Perspectives

During the midnight hour
When silence peaks in shadows
The soft sounds of the evening
Echo in unisons of inspiring crescendos

Hear the quiet peace
Of your inner self
Murmuring revelations
Of perspectives so heartfelt

Find your true essence
Surrendering to the night
As you contemplate the best vision of you
To bring forth, come the rise of morning light

*[*Title is a Six-Word Memoir]*

Hourglass Dreams

Creation of dreams
constructed in an hour
of snoozing slumber

[Haiku]

Slumbering Hour...

Slumbering hour: Dreams constructing clairvoyant creations.

[Six-Word Memoir]

The Dreaming Hour of Creation

Creation of dreams constructed
In an hour of snoozing slumber
Should be up and about my daily routines
Sandman too tempting, granting extra sleep
Allowing my mind to wander as it wonders

A dream weaver, dreams woven
Of subconsciously sent subliminal messages
Suggestions of fantasy merging with reality
Dreamcatchers catching in its tangled webs
Vividly dreamt images of realm-merged passages

What is your meaning, your symbolic references
Dreamworld scenery playing out possibilities
What signs are you sending, truths impending
Intimate details foreshadowing premonition visions
Should I have beliefs, faith… in trusting your credibilities

As I slumber away, dreaming precious secrets of life to be
Through my mind's fortune-telling crystal ball
What kind of prophecy through unveiled transparency
Is swirling within, dancing destinies tempting fated fortunes
Bringing decoded sensibilities alive
… through dreamy, clairvoyant calls

Passion Needs No Wake-up Call

Beep! Beep! Beep! Beep!
Resounds the alarm heard in your sleep
An instant shock away from sweet slumber
Strikes you like the loudest thunder
Waking you, with feet dragging
Same morning routine has you lagging
Grab a cup of coffee, caffeinated energy
Imitation passion brewed, for jobs you do uncaringly
That's your usual 9-5
You're there to work, just to get by
Alarm is needed to start your day
But what if it didn't have to be that way?

When waking from slumber, poses no threat
Alarms aren't required to be set
When passion is behind it all
Passion needs no wake-up call!
It's there! It's ready! Always on call!
Anytime from morning through nightfall
No blaring alarms to jolt you from sleep
Driven by passion, you jump to your feet!
A fire of desire, burns within you
Deep in your heart, it's your own coffee's brew
Awake with insomnia, it doesn't bother you
To follow what your heart, tells you to do

This ain't a job merely to stay on your feet
Not just a hobby you must focus to keep
It's a passion that's ready for you to take reign
Always on your mind this passion never wanes
It's the air you breathe, it keeps your soul alive
Passion needs not wait an alarm to arrive
When it's always there, behind it all
Passion needs no wake-up call

Beep, Beep, Dream Machine

Beep! Snooze. Beep! Beep! Snooze.
Button pressed, helps me sneak more
slumbering dream time.

[Haiku]

Daylight Eyes

Aurora rises with her radiating rays of light
　　Reaches out through slips of curtained apertures
　　　　Adjusting her grip to the size of lashes
　　　　Dipped in shadowy caricatures

Clutching sealed eyelids of slumber
　　　　Her blinding glow *JOLTS* sleeping beauties
　　　　　　From states of dreams and nightmares

This Goddess of Dawn
　　Snatches snoozers from Sandman's spell
　　　Whispers approach of a new day's potentialities
　　　　Like Mother Nature cradling lush gardens
　　　Coaxing eyelids to flourish and bloom open

Ignore the hoax of delusioned resting realms
　　Do not be lured by charms of latent lotuses
　　　　　Forget the fancies of future omens
　　　Forget reminders of past memories

O p e n your daylight eyes
　　Like eating PoPPeD rock candy
　　　　　　S i z z l i n g with effervescent sensations
　　　To walk with *jazzed* clarity in reality

Do not squint bewilderedly at living in the present
    Rub away crusted dust

                      The slumbering cries of
           Fantasized hallucinations unrealized

Seek growth through enlightenment
          Seize the day with an outlook
    Full of adventurous praise

Gaze in awe the magic splendor of a sunrise
          Feel an awakening through its exquisite colors
      Rainbow treasures found through reflective ponderings

Wrap yourself in sunshine's warmth
          Feel the kiss of day breezing in solace

Look at the world around you with renewed purpose
            Find the beauty in everything

While DISCOVERING your own MAGNIFICENCE

For daylight eyes witness possibilities
        Of miraculous fruitions

Nightlight eyes...
    Can only envision kaleidoscope of impossibilities

That torture and
tantalize
In revolving recurring
imageries
Where darkness harbors its forgetful
promises
Lost amongst twilight
hours

Behind smokescreened REM eyelids of...

R-apidly
　　　　　　E-choed
　　　　　　　　　M-adness

Until the coming of daybreak
S h a tt er s sanity's return

Stay alert.
　　　　　Stay awake.
　　　　　　　　　Survey life.

Daylight EYES now wide OPEN

-o-o-Skewer Trials, Failures-into Barbecued Success-o-o-

Line up life's

tests,
trials,
failures,
etc...

along a

s
k
e
w
e
r

Light up the grill

and t W i S t and t U r N that skewer

until you roast up life's tasty bits

'til they can be grilled to "perfection"

*[*Title is a Six-Word Memoir]*

* * * Kiss The Flame * * *

Deep in my soul
A fire has burned
Slowly gaining momentum
To the point of no return
Churning this yearning
In my heart of darkness
Dreams brought to light
Out of its clouded, smoke-like blindness

Seeing nothing but red
Raging reds of fury
Igniting from frustration's fire
Into blazing barriers along this dream's journey
Raging reds of fury soon transform
Into glorious, ruby red-orange flames
Of passion's perseverance through the storm

Flaring nineteen feet up into the air
Flickering fields of flames surround me
Encased, trapped, with no means of escape
My mind's rationality turns hazy
As I stand there, face to face
With the spirit of the fire that resides in my heart
In its heat, I quickly perspire

Feeling the warm breath of fire
Hearing the rhapsody of its wild flames
This fire has dared me to take action
As its flaming fiery tips, towards me take aim

Poetik Desire

It's coming right at me
Pointing its fingers as if to say
You must now choose
To stay and fight for me or run away
The choice I soon come to make
Is not to become a casualty
Fallen victim to the demise of my dream's fantasy

I... I won't let floods of water
Rain over me
I... I won't let my dreams
Be extinguished for all eternity

No!
I will no longer run away like a coward
In the face of danger
In the face of dreams unanswered
I will stay this time and fight for my dream
Fight to endure this fiery heat
Which emanates from my soul's feverish pit
Following through without retreat

Fueled by determination
Staring into red-orange eyes
I won't let the fire in me die
After I've set my eye on passion's prize
My fantasy, you see
Is to keep alive my dream's destiny
Allow it to thrive

I want to melt in the furnace
Of passion's burning embers
Lie in the midst of dangerous risks
Where taking chances, pushes me to remember
To face the faceless
To name the unnamed
To tame the untamed
And kiss the flame

Kiss the flame
Of my passion's desire
Kiss the flame
Before dreams expire
Become one with something
So dangerous, so magical
So vengeful, yet merciful
Embrace the path that my fate travels
Tiptoe through ashes of fallen dreams
Rise through the fury of fallen dreams redeemed
Kiss the flame
And be revived
Kiss the flame
So my dreams can survive

Poetik Desire

Dreamers Dream Big

Dreamers dream big
Hoping to skid
Into dreams turned reality
As dreamers strive to up the ante

[Quatrain]

Chasing Dreams

You know, for awhile now
It's been a cat and mouse chase
And you were the mouse
That scurried through my mind every day
You toyed with my emotions
You tugged at my heart strings
You ran out of my reach
You're my chasing dream

My dreaming prey
I've chased for years
Always evading
My finger-tipped spears
But soon you'll see
You were destined to be
Pinned, cornered, and devoured
By the one who's been…

Hungry, hungry for a taste of you
Hungry, hungry for a taste of you
My appetite has been building up
For oh so long, I've been craving you
Craving a bite, a nibble, a taste
Savoring morsel crumbs of your trails
This starving artist won't ever bail
And it's no surprise, 'cause I realize

Chase those dreams
Chase those dreams
Keep pushing forward
And chase those dreams
Believe in myself
Follow my heart
Chase those dreams
Don't let 'em depart

You gotta reach for the stars
And chase those big dreams
Believe in who you are
And what you can achieve
Don't you ever let others
Dictate your dreams
'Cause they can't decide
If you'll fail or succeed

Only you are the one
Who stands in your
Own way of making
Your dreams mature
Just remember to get out
Of your own way
If you ever want your dreams
To see the light of day

Believe, believe in your own self
Believe, believe in your own self
Your chasing dreams are within your grasp
Learn to have some faith, it's your passion's wealth
Have faith in the skills that you possess
To truly believe that you can achieve
Your heart's desire, your chasing dream
Made real, made true, 'cause you see it was you who...

Chased those dreams
Chased those dreams
Kept pushing forward
And chased those dreams
Believed in yourself
Followed your heart
Chased those dreams
And gave 'em their start

You had that mousetrap set
To catch scurrying dreams
You let 'em be catnapped
By you who envisioned its scheme
Waiting patiently
Through all your mishaps
Never expecting achievements
To just fall in your lap

Poetik Desire

No one could catch
This dreaming prey for you
Only you can bite
Into your dreams come true
Just lunge and capture
Those chasing dreams
And relish in delight
The taste of life's...

Rarest delicacy
Of dreams
Cooked to perfection
As you
Nibble on...
Bites of success...
As within your grip...
You now possess...
Your captured dreams

And never will you let those dreams
Go rampantly unfulfilled
Or give your dream its own liberation
Of freewill
To escape and steal the passion
You so deeply feel
For that captured dream that's now
Your succulent meal

There to satisfy your hunger
As a starving artist
Healing skeptic views you've always had
Of your own talents
Feeding you with faith and confidence
To move on forward
'Cause destinies of chasing dreams
Are never looking backwards

Have faith, have faith
That you'll catch those dreams
When you learn to stop becoming
Your worst enemy
Gain the confidence required
To maintain belief
Your heart's desires can…
Be achieved!

Catch those dreams
Catch those dreams
Just pull 'em out of
Your mind's secrecy
And share with the world
Your lustrous dream pearl
Witness appreciation
Of your dream's consummation

Poetik Desire

You're the chasing dreamer
Now in control
Of a captured dream
No longer free
To scurry away
From its destiny
Now belonging to you
The catcher of dreams!

Like a Caged Bird

*"The ultimate measure of a man is not where he stands
in moments of comfort and convenience but
where he stands at times of challenge and controversy."*

- Martin Luther King, Jr

Moon Harbors Failed Dreams

Failed shooting star wish.
Boom! Crater formed. Grief absorbed.
The moon weeps for me

[Haiku]

Improvise, Endure...

Nothing goes as expected. Improvise. Endure.

[Six-Word Memoir]

Trapped in a Hidden World

Walking through life
Blind and unguided
Standing on your own
Everything's undecided

Trapped in a hidden world
Known only by you
You try hard to escape
But there's no breaking through

Your subconscious mind
Begins to control your life
As you continue to live
Through troubles and strife

You feel out of place
Never seeming to belong
What will happen next
In a life void of a song?

Forever feeling trapped
With a mind of uncertainty
Wouldn't it be great
If life was just easy?

Still, you wander through life
Blind and unguided
Lost in a world unknown
You're left alone and stranded

Burdened

Is there anyone who can help me
Unburden all my troubles
Take away this sadness
Bring me happiness that once was?

As the days go by
Life goes on as it does
But there are times like these
Where a kind of burden builds up

Builds up so much it's overpowering
Consuming my whole being
'Til I've lost all sense of control
Sending my whole world spinning

No one seems to listen
No one understands
I'm fighting my own battle
A battle even I sometimes don't understand

Am I all alone in this?
Who else feels such pain?
Will shadows continue to hide me in the dark
As tears pour out like thundering rain?

Like a Caged Bird
[Cinquain Verses]

Held in captivity
Confined to one small space
Unable to break free
Cause I possess no key
To free me of this locked cage

Binding me
To entrapments of solitude
I have no room to fly
To explore what's outside
Beyond these metal bars I can't elude

I've become a caged bird
Determined to spread my wings
Seek a world found just beyond
These locked doors that keep me bound
Unable to reach for that golden horizon

Where I imagine with wings unclipped
Unchanged seasons of scenery
Granting me freedom to soar the open sky
To explore what's beyond a confined life
Experience a world where I'm alive and free

Carry On

How can I manage to carry on
To make it through my struggle day after day
When the emotional baggage I carry
Is an accessory I'd rather have lost or given away?

Forever stuck in the overhead compartment
That is my mind
Not to be forgotten
As I travel forward in time
Experiencing layover after layover
Halting my journey forward
This depressed state I reside in
Seeks a new scheduled destination

I need to find the strength that gives me wings
To fly into a paradise far away
Where happiness is found in abundance
Strength found in the remembrance each day
Of support that helps to keep me
Strapped in for the ride of life
Weathering turbulence
Through spoken winds of advice

For in the cockpit of life's travels
You must choose wisely the baggage you'll carry on
Stored in your mind's overhead compartment
Thoughts guide your travels beyond

Healing Scars

Scarred minds heal, unseen.
Scarred body forever wears
symbols of courage.

[Haiku]

Littered Mind...

Littering a mind plagued with confusion.

[Six-Word Memoir]

Anger's Desperation

Anger blinds, reason
is left behind, acting out
in desperation.

[Haiku]

Anger Blinds...

Anger blinds. Tears whined. Emotions misaligned.

[Six-Word Memoir]

Poeticized Can of Worms

Oh, yeah…
        You better believe
                I just opened that can
                        That can which was sealed tight
                                Of emotions marinating
                        In its tiny space of captivity
                Bursting out in full force
        Upon its release
Wiggling around
        Like a pile of worms
                Worms entangled
                        With a poetic nature
                                Airing its truest essence
                                        Careless
                        Of newfound complications
                Free to just be
        Freely exposed
    Free of its dark
Harbored
        Emotions of captivity
                Strewn about through this page
                        For you to clearly see
                                What's been locked up tight
                        Entangled with rage
                As with its release
        Comes emotional freedom
A can of worms
        Poetically revealing

A truth unknown
Now revealed to you
Uncontained
Uninhibited
For when contained
No harm is caused to anyone
Except to your own soul
As with containment
Comes internal emotional damage
Damage that when given time
To build up
To marinate in despair
It's only a matter of time
'Til that seal is infiltrated
As a can of worms
Is opened
Set free
To crawl its way out
Out of its captivity
Of preservation
Of truth ripened
Maturity given
As outbursts unleash
Emotions restrained
Harnessed in a vessel
Of a steel prison
And once given ventilation
This canned lid
Can no longer seal
What has now escaped
Been released

Poetik Desire

Emotions which have
Squirmed its way to the open
Seeking to never return
To its tiny space of captivity
As it wiggles
Entangles
In its taste of freedom

When Nothing is Everything

The house that once was a home
Is no longer a place for this family to call home
For through the wrath Mother Nature brings
This family has now lost all treasured materialistic things
Treasured invaluables now lost forever
Lost in the winds or flames or floods
Of life's unexpected disasters

Possessions once endowed
With the memories of this family's life from then and now
Are now lost reminders of a family's life lived
This family now feels trapped in a pensive state of mind
Wondering why to them Mother Nature has been so unkind

Where's the nurture of a mother's nature?
The nourishing upbringing towards a family's future?
Where once a mother's nature gave this family
A life of comfort, a sense of security
In one fail swoop of Mother Nature's unforeseen wrath
This family now stumbles along broken stones
Towards a different life's path

Broken stones of which this family steps upon and follows
Is a slow, agonizing walk taken
Through their broken-hearted limbo
Stripped of everything that defined this family as a whole
They feel the perfect life they've lived, Mother Nature now stole

Although the nurture of this mother's nature
Has flipped its guise revealing its neglectful features
The beauty found in afflictions of an anguished heart
Is discovering the reality of life's most essential parts
That which are the truest necessities of life
Composed not of materialistic delights

Yes, all treasured valuables
May have been lost in one of life's disasters
And this family feels they've lost everything
That has ever mattered
Feels they are left with nothing
Of a life they were living

Nothing left of importance
Nothing left of remembrance
Nothing left of memories
Nothing left but minds filled with worries

Worries about where this broken path
Shall lead a family now homeless
Worries about how to keep alive
The beautiful memories of the past

But in a twist of quiet reflection
Once the mind has eased from its distressed tension
The beauty found in losing everything
Is realizing you are not left with nothing
Within your soul, you discover an awakening
As you see what you are left with in the end...

Your life...
 Your family...
  and most importantly:
   love and memories...

All of which can never be replaced or erased!
For materialistic things can easily be displaced and then replaced

When the nurture of Mother Nature fails you with her wrath
Just remember she's given you the greatest blessing
As you step along your broken path
As piece by piece, you put back together
The puzzling new path you now follow
In the back of your mind, forever will you hear the echoes...

 You're alive! You made it through!
 You still have your family to stand by you...

  As long as love survives through it all
  Love is what shall pick you up, when you fall...

   Lost possessions of life's memories - matters less
   When forever in your mind they will be carried - in excess,...

   And when you seem to have lost everything,
   Remember how nothing truly can be everything!

Life's Plans...

Life's all about handling Plans B,C,D,E...

[Six-Word Memoir]

Broken by Life...

Broken by life, healed by strength.

[Six-Word Memoir]

Prescription for Guilt

Face the guilt you feel
Walk through the pain of anguish
Learn from your mistakes

[Haiku]

Guilt

G rieve what you feel guilty of/for

U nderstand why you're where you are,
      how you've reached this point

I n time you'll come to see

L ight shining at the end of guilt's shadowed tunnel

T o bring you full circle,

        guilty notions make us
    e   h
     r   u
    e   m
    h   a
   w   n,
      m a k e u s c h a n g e

[Acrostic]

Relax. Breathe...

Relax. Breathe. Things work out somehow.

[Six-Word Memoir]

A Serpentine Journey

Life never follows a straight line,
there's always twists and turns thrown in
to keep you from getting too complacent
with a "certain way of life",
just gotta pray each day and have the faith
that "this too shall pass"
if you can endure the wait for change to come.

[Free Form]

Rising Joy

Life's straight and narrow
must flow through twists and turns... joy
shall rise from sorrow.

[Haiku]

Time

Time doesn't heal wounds;
what you do with the passing
of time - is what heals

[Haiku]

Mourning Before Sun

Love and joy will rise with the morning sun
But why must I mourn, before I see morn?

When grief, depression, is allowed its course to run
Love and joy will rise with the morning sun

Wallowing in rivers of tears, 'til eyes are left barren
Manifests unclouded visions, replenished spirit
                                    - mends a heart so torn

Love and joy will rise with the morning sun
But why must I mourn, before I see morn?

[Triolet]

Dawning Dreams in Drowsy Darkness

Outside I hear the rain pouring
Sense the cool swirling winds
Although inside, dry I stay
Find showering upon me
Goosebumps of lethargic susceptibilities

Snuggled beneath fabrics of covered warmth
Feel the woven entanglements found within
The pitter patter of mental pains
Throbbing against my idle brain
Synapses of enlivenment
Fails to spark thriving connections
To lift me out of my sluggish spirit

Laid out I be
Eyes closed in silence
As one eye peeks open
Peering amidst surroundings
For dawning dreams in drowsy darkness
To awaken me with energizing calmness

Families Unite in Economic Plight
[Lai Nouveau]

When money's bound tight,
families unite -
seek change.
Thrifty theory fights
amongst who's more right -
for change -
challenges our trite
economic plight.

Though to change our life
stabs us sharp as knives -
piercing
deep with all its might -
forsaking delights,
struggling
through unwanted strifes
when money's bound tight.

Cautious, controlled lights
switch on and off life's
modern
day utilized sites
of comforted heights.
Stubborn
are we, of changed life -
families unite.

All quarreling fights
silenced day to night,
bitten
tongues hold back indicts,
switching on searchlights,
smitten
by debtor contrite
when money's bound tight.

Shining a spotlight
on fiscal termites,
expunged
habits meet rewrites
so comforted heights
are reached
once more in this life -
families unite.

Bonded in love's light,
family's strength might
just yearn
assessment, ignites
financial-matched light
to earn
fiscal freedom flight
when money's bound tight.

Gaining some foresight,
escape poor's limelight,
be rich
on soiled homesite
as overcame plights
sew stitched
hopeful-rayed sunlight -
families unite.

Learning from hindsight,
choices affect life -
arranged
for you, paying price
for a debted life -
how strange...
families unite
when money's bound tight

The Price of Life

Everything ain't 'bout
the money, except when you
need to make ends meet.

[Haiku]

Just Breathe

Life suffocates us
Despaired chokes test our strength to
Inhale... exhale.... breathe…

[Haiku]

Still, I Kept on Fighting

My world turned upside down
Couldn't tell if I was swimming to escape
Or drowning deeper in despair
Still, I kept on fighting
Emotional waves that kept crashing
'Til breath of relief resurfaced
Resuscitated ashore

[Free Form]

Life's Riptides...

Surfing life's riptides of clashing principles.

[Six-Word Memoir]

~ ~ ~ Swimming in a Sea of Debt ~ ~ ~

We're swimming in a sea of debt
Living paycheck to paycheck
Just barely can we dare to foresee
Enjoyment in many of life's luxuries

~ ~ ~ ~ ~

We're wading in the deep end
Just waiting to be pulled in
Slowing losing momentum
Are we ready to drown in the deep end?

~ ~ ~ ~ ~

We've tiptoed through the shallow waters
Splashing with joy like nothing matters
But slowly we've drifted to deeper depths
Where water is just barely kept below our heads

~ ~ ~ ~ ~

We've faltered and few times disparaged
Throughout the course of this marriage
Testing the financial waters of life
We've seen both its joys and its strife

~ ~ ~ ~ ~

Riding the calm seas
Braving the turbulent, rough seas
We've managed at times to navigate our way
Through seas of debt, surviving to see another day

~ ~ ~ ~ ~

But now we've floated to the deep end once more
Slowly closes that financial freedom door
As we kick our legs and flail our arms
Fearing drowns of debt will do us harm

~ ~ ~ ~ ~

We keep treading water with all our might
Keeping hope alive that all will turn out right
But as sharks of debt surround us to collect
We quickly realize our means of living are over met

~ ~ ~ ~ ~

Our life vest of rescue is nowhere to be found
Prepare now for the inevitable, prepare to drown
Failure to be prepared for any of life's emergencies
Leaves you plunging deeper into seas of uncertainty

~ ~ ~ ~ ~

As we begin to submerge, lacking swells of dollars
Drowning deeper into debt, there's no escaping creditors
Sinking deeper and deeper into the financial abyss
Currents tow us towards a bottomless money pit

~ ~ ~ ~ ~

Laying beneath the surface on the ocean floor
We've drifted so far from financial freedom's shore
Struggling to resurface for breaths of fresh air
'Til no longer are we swimming seas of debt in despair

The Irony of Effort

Why when others try too hard…
they fail to succeed,
fail to obtain what they've envisioned…

while for others
it comes to them too easily,
success obtained
without trials and tribulations?

Society's Economic Divide
[Haiku Verses]

Society poor
Living paycheck to paycheck
Drowning in despair

Society rich
Living lives the poor dream of
Swimming in cash flow

Society poor
Lives life with uncertainty
With each passing day

Society rich
Takes for granted "easy life"
Can't fathom hardships

No Escaping Life's Troubles

Hurling fast towards me
Choo! Choo! Life's train wreck… screeeeching!
Unable to stop

[Haiku]

Life's Afflictions...

Life's afflictions birth concepts of hope.

[Six-Word Memoir]

III
Inferiority Complex

"I am out with lanterns, looking for myself"

- Emily Dickinson

° o ° o Ball of Depression o ° o °

Lost   bounce   life
       my   for

U n m o t i v a t e d to m O v E

Curled up, **HIDES** - from life

[Haiku]

Unsolved Heartaches...

Unsolved heartaches, wearied souls, troubled anguish.

[Six-Word Memoir]

Crossroads of Doubt
[Cinquain Verses]

My life has been full of mistakes
Leading me down the wrong roads to take
With every fork in the road I face
Comes a decision made in disgrace
Unsurety leads to confidence I forsake

Always coming to the end of a road
That seems like it provides no hope
My edges are tattered
My life's become shattered
If all goes wrong, how will I cope?

For my life remains at a crossroads
Voices in my head have always echoed
The chorus of being forever flawed
Sung by anxieties dared to be outlawed
Clawing through paths so tightly narrowed

(((Fears)))

Fears can get the best of you
Consuming your whole being
But you've got to be strong and pull through
Past its ever-powerful feeling

When situations arise
Where fear presents itself
You'll feel all tied up in knots
How can you control yourself?

The trick you see
Is plain as can be
You have to be brave
Break through the waves

With confidence gained
You'll see through the rain
Only the strong survive
Hope keeps them alive

So, in the toughest of times
Look deep into your soul
To find your inner strength
To keep you feeling whole

Stand tall and be strong
Cast your fears aside
And brighter days will prevail
If you keep faith on your side

Poetik Desire

^v-^v-^v- Peer Pressure -v^-v^-v^

With so much peer pressure
    Surrounding each one of us

It's no wonder why adolescent life
    Is complicated for all of us

        Pressure is put on everyone
            To try several different things

        Pressure to try sex, drugs,
            And other bad things

It's amazing to see the decisions
    That others make for themselves

Cause the majority of us go through with it
    Yet there's only a few who don't

        So why is it so easy
            To be pushed into these things

        Why is it so hard
            For so many of us to decide

On what we want in life
    What we want for ourselves

Not to please those others
    Who don't rule your life

        Just try to keep control
            Don't sway from your morals

        Do what's right for you
            Don't let peer pressure control you

Wrestling with Myself

Own worst enemy
Never winning battles, when...
Wrestling with myself

[Haiku]

Self-Critical Vilifications...

Interminable self-critical vilifications detain desired self-imaging.

[Six-Word Memoir]

Always Self-Critical...

Always more self-critical than self-assured, self-loved...

[Six-Word Memoir]

Inferiority Complex

At times I feel like I'm faced
With this inferiority complex
Like I won't amount to anything
Never knowing what to expect

Even though I know what my strengths are
It's my weaknesses that overpower me
It's what I worry about the most
Despite the best of my abilities

Sometimes I get so frustrated
With the kind of life I live
Feeling there's no place I fit in
I just wish I had more to give

I just want to experience
More of what life has to offer
But it seems with my inferiority complex
I'll never receive that offer

Positively Pessimistic

My convincingly obscured vision of my current state of life
Examines how shriveling success can rise through fortunate strife

Where the absence of success becomes a blesséd failure
And fruitless fruition scrutinizes questionable behavior

For life taught me through brainwashed lessons
of contented anguish
How strife ornately simplifies fortunes of the impoverished

Where thrifty lifestyles have been wealthily paid
In extravagances of life's most valued treasures freely attained

Where the best things in life forfeits monetary earnings
For blind enlightenment of life's most priceless yearnings

As tightly held in my slippery grip is life's silhouette strings
Guiding lifestyles of perfected imperfections
through its puppeteering

Where I am that puppet clumsily dancing with tiptoed grace
Through conveniently placed obstacles I must evadingly face

Poetik Desire

Expecting an amazing phenomenon of accidentally
aiming on purpose
To land swiftly upon life's revelations through my
unrehearsed dance steps

Carelessly performing with ascertained uncertainty
The shuffle dance of unmarked paths leading to my destiny

Paths littered with self-revealing contemplations
Bedded within a simple phrase's complex cross-examination

Is this glass voluminously void of liquid containment?
In other words, do I see this glass as half full or half empty?

The mirrored inequalities of such a question's reflective responses
Obviously reveals my vague understanding of how I
approach life's bridges

When seen half full, optimistically I fail to hesitate upon crossing
When seen half empty, pessimistically I'm certain
to abandon my journey

So, while I'm positively pessimistic
I'm also opposingly optimistic

Because I'm positive the way I've come to view life
Exaggerates all tangent aspects of its hype

Lucky enough to expect the worst of the best
While jinxed with receiving the best of the worst

Now unconvinced perception of my future life state
Fathoms how fortunate failure becomes a fundamental trait

Where an abundance of failure can lead to bléssed success
Fruitful imperfections surrounding each answer confessed

Silent Storms Within

Still waters run deep
Hiding violent storms brewing
Waits to break surface

[Haiku]

Fragile Strength

Life's

s
  T
 o
  r
M

can w e a k e n

STRONG souls; their

    l
  e   t
 h   e
s   r
 n   e
u   d

solitude s e e k s *REFUGE*

[Monostich]

Unspoken Chaos

She tries to flourish with all her might
To grow from the shadows and welcome the light
The despair and anguish felt
The uncertainties of fear that melt
Within the fractured cracks of her soul
Seeps a deep sadness of longing that takes its toll
...awaiting to be renewed and made whole

        She closes her eyes
        And dares to whisper a wish
        To be pulled from her self-wreckage
        Before her spirit shall perish
        Hoping her message will take flight
        Upon feathered hope
        ...to reach those who can help her cope

Solitude's deteriorating effects is all she knows
As she quietly surrenders to her unspoken chaos
But this frame of mind is not sustainable
She must find peace and solace in what's obtainable
...to build her strength, become unbreakable

Save Me From Me

How can I save the future me
From the past me
That can't get past the present me
To move onwardly
Without interweaving
All existential parts of me?

How do I save me from me
When I am my own worst enemy
Fighting demons
Cursing self
A dichotomy entanglement
Between self-image
And impressionistic view by others?

In one instance
I'm positively in love with myself
Loving this part and that
Relishing in the glory
Of the spirit of me
Seeing the good I possess
Confidence confessed

But in my days of despair
When sunshine fades
And gloomy skies blanket
Perspectives of this self-portrait
Feeling less than perfect
Seeing only the weight
Of my imperfections

Disgracefully, I degrade myself
Look down on my worth
Seeing only what darkness
Wants to cloak me in sadness
To sulk in pity
Feeling not so pretty
Inner voices so damaging
I hear crickets of the night
More clearly spoken than

Crickets of subconscious advice
How a hush of silence
Veils internal monologues
Of self-reassuring support
Hearing only harsh soliloquies
Recited repeatedly

Poetik Desire

Loudly speaking in tongues to self
Parts of speech that lose all meaning
Trains of thought constantly derailing
Spun out of control
Like a Tasmanian devil
I create my own cyclone
Of self-destructiveness
Unable to break free of
Internal storms
Full of thundering defeat

Unsure of how to see
Where the light of day will break through
Who will it be
That can save me from me?
Do I turn to you
Or is it all up to me?

Finding Light in the Shadows
[Pantoum]

Life can get discouraging
Lost in clouds of darkness
Unsure of how to break free
The tight claustrophobic-like ambience

Lost in clouds of darkness
Searching for light in the shadows
The tight claustrophobic-like ambience
Holds you in its binding grip

Searching for light in the shadows
A pocket of light breaks through the dark
Holds you in its binding grip
Rays of hope shining down upon you

A pocket of light breaks through the dark
A rare moment arriving when least expected
Rays of hope shining down upon you
Lifting spirits, courageous encouragements found

A rare moment arriving when least expected
Life's struggling obstacles leads to triumph
Lifting spirits, courageous encouragements found
Proven worth discovered in living boldly

Life's struggling obstacles leads to triumph
Patience rewards trust in having faith
Proven worth discovered in living boldly
Belief in yourself should never be forgotten, even when…

Patience rewards trust in having faith
Clearing dark clouds, revealing expanse of unlimited skies
Belief in yourself should never be forgotten, even when…
Life can get discouraging

Grounded Fears...

Grounded fixated fears became soaring strength.

[Six-Word Memoir]

Doubting Self...

Doubting self opens insightful, questionable self-reflections.

[Six-Word Memoir]

Changing Mindsets...

Changing colors... changing self... changing mindsets.

[Six-Word Memoir]

Refurbished Perspectives...

Refurbished perspectives furnish psyche's serene disposition.

[Six-Word Memoir]

Think Happy...

Think happy. Smile your worries away.

[Six-Word Memoir]

Clear Your Mind
[Anaphora]

Clear your mind,
     forget what others say
Clear your mind,
     live life your own way

               Clear your mind,
                    don't care what others think
               Clear your mind,
                    your life is yours to ink

Clear your mind,
     permission need not be granted
Clear your mind,
     you set your own boundaries

               Clear your mind,
                    don't let in outside influences
               Clear your mind,
                    or life's not of your own choices

Clear your mind,
     be rid of tainted thoughts
Clear your mind,
     peace of mind is sought

               Clear your mind,
                    know what is your truth
               Clear your mind,
                    be less confused

                                                Poetik Desire

Clear your mind,
      appear how you choose to be
Clear your mind,
      begin to live life carefree

             Clear your mind,
                no need to change your personality
             Clear your mind,
                you are who were born to be

Clear your mind,
      see how life flows with ease
Clear your mind,
      life is now yours to seize

             Clear your mind,
                don't worry what others say or think
             Clear your mind,
                remember your life is yours to ink

Break Through

There's always something
    In my way
        I'm looking up
            But not for hope

      But waiting for something
         To fall in front of me
            As I wobble along
                Life's thin tightrope
Obstacles confine me
    To its blockade
        I feel I have
            No room to breathe

      As I lose my balance
         Find my inner strength
            This life's restricting armor
                Must be unsheathed
I'm gonna break through the fiercest
    Powerful storms
        See the light of day
            Through the pouring rain

      As dark clouds fade
         Giving way
            Light to shine through my darkness
                Shielding me from the pain

I'm gonna break through a life
  Defined by limits
    Find the faith
      To let nothing stand in my way

    My first responsibility
      Is to myself
        To break through my hardships
        To a brighter day
The longest journey
  Begins with a single step
    A step moving forward
      To what meets me on the other side

    For everything has an opposite
      A Yin to its Yang
        Believing there's more to life than this
        Is the push I need to survive
I must take a stand…
  For myself, for my dreams
    There is hope…
      There is help I can find…

    I must believe in myself
      Love myself enough
        To live a better life
        Than the one I've been assigned

I'm gonna break through the fiercest
      Powerful storms
          See the light of day
              Through the pouring rain

        The dark clouds will fade
          Giving way
              Light to shine through my darkness
                Shielding me from the pain
I'm gonna break through this life
      Defined by limits
          Find the faith
              To let nothing stand in my way

        For my first responsibility
          Is to myself
              To break through my hardships
              To a brighter day
To break through, break through
      To find that light of day
          To break through, break through
          To find my own way

Inspired by the movie "Precious"

Poetik Desire

Held Captive to Forgiveness

[Villanelle]

No longer be held captive
Truths of insecurities, I shall unconceal
Myself – I can forgive

Hostage to rewinds of mistakes relived
Stop repeating the same spiel
No longer be held captive

Once a reactor, spoken out with angered motive
Pockets frustrations, undermining how I feel
Myself – I can forgive

Bad mom syndrome challenges my perspectives
Discard negative self-talk, confidence appealed
No longer be held captive

Denounce degraded self-worth introspectives
Acquiesce to put self first and reveal...
Myself – I can forgive

Learning to "let it go", a "moving on" persuasive
Realizing guilt can be healed
No longer be held captive
Myself – I can forgive

I Am More...

I am more than I appear.

[Six-Word Memoir]

Dawn of New Self...

Dawn of new self ripens gradually.

[Six-Word Memoir]

The Quiet Bloom of Self

Expansion of self-discoveries
Comes from investigative meditative insight
Under silenced blankets of curtained eyes

[Free Form]

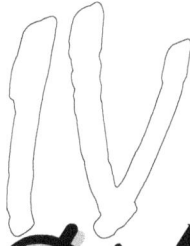

IV
Nostalgic Remembrance

"Embrace the change, no matter what it is;
once you do, you can learn about the
new world you're in and take advantage of it."

- Nikki Giovanni

Bittersweet Paradox of Change

Life is about change
That's painful or beautiful
Most moments are both

[Haiku]

Grown-Up Tantrums

Life makes us grown-ups
Have childish tantrums too
Who needs a time out?

[Haiku]

Joy of Childhood

So young and naive

    So curious yet brave

        So joyous and full of life

            F U N is what they crave

They'll s *P i N* around in circles

    Run 'til their energy is gone

        They'll get UP   when they F

                A

                 L

                  L

        And continue on and on

Their innocent eyes

    Can see no wrong

        They view this life

            As one BIG happy song

The JOY of childhood

    Is one that's unmatched

        It's an era of life…

        Adults sometimes wish to have back

Child vs. Adult Mindset

As a child, I...
was carefree, less worry, bold.
As adult... fears change.

[Haiku]

Mixed Maturities...

Adult expectations. Childlike mentality. Mixed maturities.

[Six-Word Memoir]

Childhood Regression

I'd like to regress, transgress
Back to my childhood days
When life was much simpler, chipper
Focusing on life in more enjoyable ways

Living life carefree, just be
Free of the real world's binding chains
Free of emotional, financial
Accrued baggage of life's indebted migraines

To have my eyes relit, in excitement
As no real obstacles dare cross my path
Running free, in the wind's breeze
Impermeable to real life's wrath

Finding joy of laughter, in life's chapters
Recapturing an eagerness to turn life's page
Searching to capture the same wonder, under
A youthful guise of innocent dreams to engage

Dreams untainted, unacquainted
With the cruelty of life's harsh let downs
Daring to follow pipe dreams, to its extreme
'Til real life denies those dreams be crowned

Escaping with ease, responsibilities
Of life, its grip, adults stay handcuffed to
Full of so much energy, spontaneity
Bidding adieu to all of life's issues

Why can't adults regress, transgress
Back to childhood days
When life was much simpler, chipper
Focusing on life in more enjoyable ways?

Backwards Glimpse, Forward Leaps

Reflected visions

Of life rewound in reverse

Limited focus

Look forward with wide-eyed views

Trade regrets, trust faithed futures.

[Tanka]

Nostalgic Remembrance
[Pantoum]

Before we realized, it may all one day... eventually disappear
Back in the day, we lived the good ole times of yester years
A time when everything of present-day prominence
Has now become memories of nostalgic remembrance

Living those good ole times, back in the days of yester years
Things of future popularity, were just beginning to appear
Before becoming memories of nostalgic remembrance
We reveled in those carefree moments of life's simplistic-nance

When things of future popularity, began to appear
We were learning how to step into that next otherworldly frontier
Reveling in carefree moments of a then, more simplistic life
Before those simple enjoyments were transcended by a techy life

As we learned how to step into that next other worldly frontier
We soon left behind, what's become nostalgic remembrance revered
As a more technological lifestyle transcends simple enjoyments
We fear forgetful forfeits of those yester year fragments

As too soon is left behind, reverence of nostalgic remembrance
For each era's leading trends of future present-day prominence
Though we fear forgetful forfeits of fragments of yester year
We are forced to embrace innovations of progression's premiere

As each era's leading trends of future present-day prominence
Is given life, pushing fragments of yester year into nostalgic silence
We're forced to embrace innovations of progression's premiere
Until we realize those too, will one day... eventually disappear

Poetik Desire

Life's Unexpected Diagnosis

Life can seem so day to day
So routine with not much change
But then one day can change your life
You'll begin to see things in a brand-new light

The day that's changed our life and yours
Was when we found out you had an illness with a cure
It's funny, you see, how life can change
So suddenly and at a child's young age

You were fine as can be, so healthy and vibrant
With no worries of sickness, life was pleasant
But then one day, you started getting sick
We thought it was the common cold, but we were tricked

Now we're in the hospital, where days have turned to weeks
Trying to make you feel better with several different treatments
As I sit here and ponder these past events unraveled
Realizing how life will begin its new travel

A travel down the winding road to recovery
With lots of love and support from all those who love you dearly
From this point on, life will never be the same
But as long as you're still here with us…

It's worth playing life's unexpected game!

Counting Your Blessings Within Momentous Occasions

In any given moment, time stands still...

A moment of sweetness   - - A moment of sadness
A moment of surrealness   - - A moment of madness

A moment of life given   - - A moment of life taken
A moment of life forgiven   - - A moment of life reawakened

A moment of love realized   - - A moment of compassion shared
A moment of dreams revised - - A moment of being scared

In any of life's moments
Instantaneously, time stands still
Allowing a moment for one to pause...

To count blessings within momentous standstills

While frozen in time
We reflect on momentous situations
We stop to find the hidden meaning
Within these thought-provoking translations

We may ask...
Why me?   How did this happen?
Why now?   What should I do?
What plan should be put to action?

Other times, this moment
Is a moment of joy
Of realizing how much you've been blessed
How life can be filled with moments to enjoy

Whichever of life's moments
Causes you to freeze in your tracks
In silent reverie...

Count your blessings through each momentous impact

[*Title is a Six-Word Memoir]

Life Paused...

One moment. Life paused. Blessings counted.

[Six-Word Memior]

Your Heroed Amulet, Beacon of Light
[Six Word Lines]

When troubles seem like they're never-ending
Comfort sought through acts of befriending
Have faith in my open arms
In your hour of needed charms

I'll be your guiding strength unfeared
Easing your pain with love endeared
Feel anew holding my supportive hand
Your restorative hero, here I stand

Lighting your way through darkened shadows
To brighter days upon you bestows
Love surrounding and lifting your spirits
Never alone, for I'm your amulet

*[*Title is a Six-Word Memoir]*

Poetik Desire

A Caring Volunteer's Gift of Healing

Parents of children routinely hospitalized
Often have different hardships to face
For here we are, day in and day out
Taking our children to a now familiar place
A familiar place linked to treatments galore
In hopes of finding some kind of cure
A familiar place which can sometimes seem scary
But not if we can find the right people in a hurry

They're the ones who are there
When we need a helping hand
To brighten our spirits
Like only they can
Bringing laughter and smiles
To our children's lives
Making them feel like
They no longer have to hide

Cause in times like these
Where the days can be long
Schedules becoming routine
Sometimes unexpectedly all wrong
It can be a struggle on the parent's part
To be the one to keep their child's spirits up
When we, the parent, sometimes feel
What we may have left to give is just not enough

But that's where you come in
You, the Volunteer
You're our special friend that we can count on
To bring the children lots of cheer
You give your time to these children
To play with them, listen to their needs
To ensure that their time spent here is a pleasant one
And that my friend is one very special good deed

So from one parent to one special volunteer,
I'd just like to say thank you!

Thank you for your caring heart and good spirits
And for all that you take the time to do
You are special, that much is true
Cause it's seen in how much our children love you!

Strengthened Hearts...

Strengthened hearts surviving through courageous odds.

[Six-Word Memoir]

Surviving Life...

Surviving life, impassioned to flourish... thrive.

[Six-Word Memoir]

Fantasized Reality

Reality bites!
Time to escape, fantasize
How my life should be

[Haiku]

Legendary Narratives...

Fantasy of reality living legendary narratives.

[Six-Word Memoir]

Hope Emerging...

Hope emerging from adversity's somber embrace.

[Six-Word Memoir]

Poetik Desire

~*~*~ A World of Dreams ~*~*~

There's a place that you dream of
Where dreams can come true
A place where imagination
Can be magical for you

It's a world full of dreams
Fulfill your heart's desire
Wish upon a shining star
Travel to that magical empire

Escape from reality
For just this one moment in time
To find the world you've dreamed of
A world where everything is fine

Your closest ones surround you
The magic has just begun
There's that sparkle in your eyes
As you live your dream of fun

Dreams of fairytales and magic
Are all within your sight
Whimsical characters and rides
All your wishes come to life

In this magical world of dreams
Feel like you're right at home
For you've come a long, long way
To find this special world you've always known

*** Dedicated to my daughter diagnosed with Leukemia at 2 ½ years old
in 2004. She has been considered "cancer-free" since then.

This poem was inspired by her wish granted by the Make-A-Wish Foundation
to visit the Princesses at Disney World in 2007 when she was 4 years old!

Dreams Can Come True

When it seems like your world
Is crumbling apart
And you have no love
Left in your heart
When everything in life
Just seems to go wrong
Sit back and relax
And listen to a song

If you think dreams and fantasies
Are all you have left
Better think again
There's no need to fret
For anything in life
Can be achieved
Never say it won't happen
It will if you believe

When you give up hope
And don't care anymore
You'll get all depressed
And won't be yourself anymore
Just have faith
There are things you can do
You just need to remember
That dreams can come true

V
Rainbow in the Clouds

"Be a rainbow in someone else's cloud."

- Maya Angelou

| : | Two-Way Street | : |

Relationships formed in life involve a two-way street conjunction
You can't be focused to proceed in just one isolated direction
You have no power to boast one-way streets can form connections

Cause streets of life are paved towards intents of a driven purpose
Don't get side-swiped, traveling opposite lanes with blindness
Or you'll fail to see how feasible connections to merge are missed

For relationships to work, "give-and-take" has to occur
'Cause two can't both steer behind the wheel as chauffeured driver
Nor can both be so laid back riding as traveling passenger

As passenger demands to be the back seat driver of life
Heeding passenger's commands is the driver's routine plight
But watch out! Head-on collisions may become an imminent sight

Learn to yield cautiously, dare to take risked detours
As uncertainty tempts you to push the pedal to the floor
Riding in your own lane, hear the engine roar

As you take that chance to remove your cruise control
Steering clear of your lane of choice as you coast to a roll
Turning, speeding through a journey in the opposite lane you stole

Driving on auto-pilot without any guidance
Obeying signs and signals of this relationship's license
Discovering your traction through any two-way street mergence

Poetik Desire

Sailing Compass of Friend-Ships
[Haiku Verses]

Navigating through
waters of life, this friend-ship
steers our travels

As side by side, we
co-captain our vessel, through
high or waking seas

Our friend-ship sails
uncompassed directions, through
all apparent winds

As through each other
prevails as buoys, safe when
friend-ship's lost its drift

A Friendship Personified

Your ear of compassion
My sounding board
There to hear all my troubles
As from my soul they pour
Absorbing my anguish
Eager to hear if all is well
As through all the good and bad
Your ear befriends all words I speak or yell

        Your lips of truth
        Mouth words of encouragement
        Words of understanding
        As from my lips come emotions I vent
        Telling it like it is
        Your lips say what I need to hear
        In response to my life's twists and turns
        Never fearing how harsh or sincere

Your hands of comfort
Caress with ease to calm my nerves
Catching me before I fall
When insanity lurks round that emotional curve
You swerve me from any nervous breakdowns
As you wrap me in the warmth of your hugs
In the arms of one who understands me
Ensures me, through you, I'll feel loved

Your eyes are witness
To what I may be blind to see
My actions, my choices
Through you, I experience who I appear to be
Seeing my reflection
There in your eyes
Challenges me to re-evaluate my state of being
Without having to question why

Seeking Solace

When times get tough

And you've had enough

A break you'll take

For your own sake

Take a deep breath

Your sanity will be kept

Relax and sit back

Or take a short nap

Friends will listen
To how you've been
Release your tension
Don't keep it in

Find me here

To help you through fear

Standing by you

Through all the hullabaloo

Calm yourself down

No need to frown

Cause it's been awhile

Since I've seen your smile

Don't Give Up Hope

When your life seems hard
With the obstacles you face

As you try to find a job
But the door shuts in your face

Don't give up hope
Just keep on trying

It'll take awhile
Though you feel like dying

Don't let these obstacles
Throw you down

Stand up and be strong
There's no need to frown

Your life will be worth living
As time passes on

So don't throw away your life
Since right now things are wrong

Remind yourself that I, and others,
Will always be here for you

To be that shoulder to cry on
To be your box of tissues

With assurance, promise you'll try
To do your best each day

Be strong, be proud, be confident
Be the best in every way

Soon you'll see that glimmer of light
Shining through your dark, gloomy clouds

Your life WILL become brighter
This, to you, I vow

So, hold your head high
Don't give up hope

As you climb back up
To the top of life's slope

Soaring Butterfly
[Triolet]

Spread my wings, become a butterfly
Come out from the shadows that once hid me
Confidently show my true self, uncertainties denied

Spread my wings, become a butterfly
Thanks to all who helped me soar to the sky
Reaching dreams on the horizon so daringly, gracefully

Spread my wings, become a butterfly
Come out from the shadows that once hid me

Uncertain Storms

[Prose]

For through all the uncertainty,
of one thing I'm certain...
the sun will once again shine
through the passing storm,
my lifeline once more...
realigned.

Drenched in tears
of stressed-out fears,
these challenges I must face
through each coming year,
become the memories
which strengthen the bonds
which once kept me broken.

Basking in the sun
of life's resolutions,
all problems stemmed
from a raging storm
are brought into light
to be reformed.

Rising from the ashes,
reaching for the stars,
mistaken dreams fragmented
shall become destiny's
tokened heirloom of promises
spoken to overcome epidemics
of melancholic states
we're often drawn to mimic.

Poetik Desire

Sanctuary of Weakened Strength

Even the strongest can become weakened
    Needing the once weakened souls they uplifted
    To reciprocate paid forward dues

Roles now shifted
    As I call upon you
    For solicited support
    To become a strengthened force
    Of necessitated guidance

Be the foundational groundwork
    That builds me up once more
    Returns to me to my solid
    Strongly built structure
    That can once more house the needy

Ability to give shelter
    Be that safe haven
    To weather weakened souls
    Through all of life's storms

But this strong structure of empathy
    Can form blistering cracks
    Can also be beaten down
    Begin to crumble
    From being the shielder of external storms
    As sanctuaried escape to others

Begin to collapse under pressure
> From all the storms that brew internally
> Creating tornadic emotional whirlwinds

But where can I seek refuge?
> Where can my soul be rescued?
> Where can I dodge my lightning attacks
> My thundering thoughts
> My precipitating emotions
> Clouding me
> In my unsheltered solitude?

How can I request comforting support?
> When I am perceived
> As the doer for others
> The sacrificer of self-preservation
> That appears free of turbulent battles

But I am the ultimate pretender
> Imposter of okayness
> Able to plaster a smile
> A permanent fixture
> To mask how strong
> I truly stand before you

When my path should falter
When life's curveballs swing at me
I'm not the batter up
That can strike a home run victory
As the sole runner
To outrun my troubles
As a one-man team

No! Don't let my Pisces nature
Of sensitive sympathetical tendencies
Fool you into thinking
I can always swim through life carefree
I, too, need strengthening
When I flap like a fish out of water
Through weakened states of mind
Through various stages of this life

Strengthened by...
Supportive arms stretched out
Embracing surrounding warmth
Squeezing comfort throughout my whole being

Strengthened by...
Extended ears openly listening
Without judgment
Without interjection
Without need for vocalized attention
Just listen with caring intentions
To allow me to vent my troubles
Vent what I, too, have of struggles

Strengthened by...

      Your voice of reason to counteract
      When my cricket's conscience
      Stumbles, hangs...
      On the edge of my shoulder
      Unable to find the words of advice
      To pull me back up from fallen grace
      Whisper encouragements
      Upon my sulking face

Even the strongest need to be strengthened

      By the once weakened souls they uplifted
      To reciprocate paid forward dues

For when my strength becomes weak

      When I feel the need to call upon you
      Please realize that in that moment...
      "I don't got it"...
      "I'm not gonna get my own self through this"

I now need something in return

      I never ask, but when I do
      When something's wrong with me...

Can I turn to you as my place of sanctuary?

Poetik Desire

Your Confidence in Me Fueled My Success

For me, you never…
Doubted my abilities
In me, you believed

[Haiku]

Rainbow in the Clouds

I need life's rainbows
To brighten my cloudy days
Pull me far away from
These blanketed skies of gray
Blessing upon me
Protection from imminent storms
Colorful rays of hope revealing
That all will be right come morn

As life's stormy clouds
Come rolling on in
Pouring raindrops of fear
Obscuring my vision
Possibility of hope
These foreboding moments enshroud
Til I find what I seek
A rainbow in those clouds

Whose rays of light are always
Within view
My path to find that light
Is for me to choose
To go it alone
And become my own rainbow of hope
Or to search for other rainbows
Who can help me cope

Do I go around this cloud
With hesitation
Careful not to provoke this storm
As I tiptoe around its edges
Hoping its omnipotent
Presence won't intensify
'Til I've discovered assistance
From a rainbow ally

Or do I push through this cloud
With determination
To become my own ray of hope
My own inspiration
With courage to stand my own ground
No longer running for cover
Seek that rainbow within me
To break through these storms that hover

Whichever path that I may choose
To cast out these stormy clouds
The light is always there
To be sought after and found
And once I've found that rainbow
In the clouds of life's despairs
I hope I've learned to rise above those clouds
Aspire to become something so rare...

A ray of light that shines hope,
Through even the stormiest of days
Protection found beneath
My colorful archways
Now look up and see
Your gray skies cleared
For I, your rainbow in the cloud
Says "Never fear, I am here!"

VI
Painted Destiny

"It is not in the stars to hold our destiny but in ourselves."

- William Shakespeare

Destined Birthright

The beginning stages of the creation of life
Blesses us with our destined birthright
Genetic disposition influences our fate
Unique talents become a sought-after trait

Wrapped all snug, born out of the seed of love
Eyes of wonder seek guidance from above
Of ways to hone our talents when we've grown
This destined birthright that is ours to own

What makes us special, makes us unique
Why be like everyone, why not be mystique?
An aura of mystery surrounds your techniques
Of mystic muses seducing your talents to speak

Silenced in awe, subconscious speculations
Begin to speak volumes of receptive revelations
How something so big, so grand, and so right
Comes in a small package, this little seed of life

Packed full of surprises unique to each seed
Blessed with a destined birthright for us to heed
Chosen and given to us unknowingly
We must accept what makes us each so special and see...

How a rite of passage to our path of talents
Unlocks in realization of our own brilliance
Once it has been accepted, believed, and honed
Destined birthrights become yours to own

Poetik Desire

Passion's Pursuit

Best way
to find success
is to seek pursuit of
that which is your heart's passion
captured.

[Cinquain]

A Gifted Talent

You don't find your gift
of talent wrapped, delivered...
your gift, it finds you!

[Haiku]

Painted Destiny

Like a blank canvas, we paint our own destiny
The big picture presented is yet unknown
Its fate determined by the actions and thoughts
Of its artist who remains in sole control

Is its destiny predetermined, subconsciously known
Or is its fate a result of beautiful mishaps?
Are the choices made, distinct and clear
Or unpredictably more obscure, unreal, abstract?

In the winds of expectation, through clouds of white
Comes the conception of an idea awaiting to become
A true work of art through opportunities to fabricate
A brilliant masterpiece as its final outcome

The composition of our painted destiny
Directs our eyes to places of scrutiny
A visual representation that gives us clarity
The path to follow, imagination has foreseen

Lines drawn become our outlined aspirations
Straight, curved, heavy, light, soft, hard – a blended mixture
Representing movement, the dance of our destiny
Steps taken to help mold our future

Painted tones in varying shades of our endeavors
Are impressions of what is soon left behind
In the darkness of uncertainty, shadows give meaning
To what we've seen along the way, which once held us confined

Poetik Desire

Pockets of light are the breath of fresh air
A brightness revealing a truth untold
A glimmer of light shining our way
To our place in the world for us to grab hold

An emotional rollercoaster effect of rises and falls
Are depicted through colors, textures, and tones
As we try to color our aspirations inside the lines
Mistakes are bound to be made, it's how destiny learns to grow

Into the big picture presented to us in the end
With textures giving memory to emotions felt on this journey
The intensity of color signifying strength and purity
In the desires conceived of our painted destiny

$. $. $. A Priceless Gift . $. $. $

Passion is a pricele$$ gift

Of intrinsic *VALUE*

Not m-e-a-s-u-r-e-d in dollar ign

But in moments

Of *STOLEN* gasps of *AIR*

JuMpStArTiNg

A passionate *bEaTiNg* heart

Ride of My Life

I'm queued up for the warm-up
Shuffling through life's exciting flight of
Vexing challenges, my will of patience
Tested to advance through any hindrance

Oh, I'm ready to let loose and leave behind
Any excuse that I've been previously assigned
Ain't gonna refuse migration through this line
To journey in truce through destiny's rollercoaster design
Give me clearance to get strapped in for the ride
Adrenaline released once I've come to decide
To step aboard, oh how these butterflies just won't subside

As I prepare…

For the ride of my life, up a slow, steep climb
To follow this dream, seems like a lifetime
Hearing creaks of regret pulling on time wasted
Pondering what's along this journey crafted

As I take that first deep plunge
Soaring into life's looped challenges
Seems no easy way out of destiny's carriage
This ride of my life's become more than I've imagined
Hanging on tight, breathless, I'm scared to speak
As destiny gravitates me towards its reach
Resting upon still hills above clouds of dreams

Now I've reached…

The peak of opportunity's
Ride building up in intense speed
Looping wild curves until I've reached the end
Worried what may lurk around each bend

  Scared to swerve off, for the fall is extreme
  With eyelids closed, I believe in my dreams
  To keep me on track where I'm destined to be
  Fighting the urge to surrender in screams
  As I soar, swerve, loop through the ride of my life
  Daring to climb up incredible heights
  Plunging to the end, full of contented fright

  Accepting…

Excitement that my world once lacked
Tasting bits of its adrenaline attack
Though scared to embark on the ride of my life
I dare to experience destiny's soaring flight

  My faith was tested in destiny's design
  I was taught to have courage to step back in line
  And allow future destinies and me to entwine…

Let's Ride Again!

Poetik Desire

Luck Journeys...

Luck journeys where charms are found.

[Six-Word Memoir]

Luck Rewards...

Luck rewards optimistic views, positive convictions.

[Six-Word Memoir]

Wishful Thinking...

Positive, wishful thinking grants luck-filled possibilities.

[Six-Word Memoir]

∞ The Alchemy of Luck ∞

Positive convictions…   convincing
Myself to believe…   in possibilities
Optimistic views…   dreaming
To become realistic…   true feasibility

Luck - is it a false belief?

Luck - is it just superstitious?

Luck - is it fated, destined?

Luck - is it crafted, surreptitious?

Luck is whatever you desire
In how you wish to define its reasoning
Often defined as coincidental contingencies
Hinged hopes of enlightened envisioning

Lucky Spirits...

Lucky spirits lie between crossed fingers.

[Six-Word Memoir]

Natural Luck...

Luck: Whatever happens naturally, reasonably, fatefully.

[Six-Word Memoir]

Blossomed Fruitions...

Right moment blossomed fruitions, patience rewarded.

[Six-Word Memoir]

Right Moment of Opportunity

A moment in time
To discover what's meant to be
A hope, wish, desire
Something only held within a dream
Confined in secrecy
Lingering on edges
Of cloudy, silver linings
Yet to be realized pledges

The right moment
The right time
For circumstances
To come together aligned
Fragmented jigsaw pieces
Perfect fit found
Completes the puzzle
Right moment astounds

Giving you a breather
Weighted burdens lifted
Sought after promotional rewards
Opportunity gifted
The right moment
Awaits the perfect timing
What's meant to be
Comes to those who keep climbing

Poetik Desire

Climbing to reach great heights
Climbing out from deep despair
Do not miss right moment's key
Unlocking your life's needed repair
Keep reaching, dreaming, believing
Right moment blossoms fruitions
For those with patience are rewarded
Hard work, luck… awaits right time and course of action

Life's Puzzle Pieces...

Life's puzzle pieces finally coming together.

[Six-Word Memoir]

Life's Revision...

Life: A constant process of revision.

[Six-Word Memoir]

Experiences... Moments...

Experiences... moments... make our lives glow.

[Six-Word Memoir]

Poetik Desire

New Creation: Challenges Change, Encourages Enlightenment

A transformation
Something envisioned
Becomes a new creation
Along a changing path
Of new beginnings

A journey forged
Through finding new meaning
In ideas of life, love, and work

New identities and relationships blossom
New discoveries, new inventions
Spark inspiration's flowing momentum

To be challenged
To leave old problems behind

To bring to light
Obstacles overcome... redefined
It's a willingness...
to change one's self...
To bring about change in the world

To have faith in a HIGHER POWER

To trust instincts
to
follow
a
detour
that leads to rebirth and forgiveness

REVITALIZATION and re-creations

Encouraging ENLIGHTENMENT

To follow the challenging path of

a NEW CREATION

[*Title is a Six-Word Memoir]

Paused Passions Awaiting Activation

Life happens, deferred
passions actively seeking
inspired impulse

[Haiku]

Reanimate Talents...

Reanimate fallow talents as if unforgotten.

[Six-Word Memoir]

Just Do It...

Just do it! Conceive. Believe. Achieve.

[Six-Word Memoir]

A Search for Lost Poetic Perch

Though life has turned
Insanely busy
Orbiting such responsibilities
Has left me a bit dizzy
Where I find
I'm steadily searching
For my lost
Poetic perching
Drowning in a sunken ship
Of my passion's calling
Where resuscitation of inspiration
Has been stalling

The murky swells of life
Has stilled its waters
I must find peace in ripples
Amongst the calm of chaotic clatter
Where a breath of fresh air
Cleanses my choked expressions
So that I may now speak
Of rescued revelations
Behold what has lingered
In my steadied search
As found time illustrates return
To my once lost poetic perch

Dusting Off Repurposed Talents

My destined purpose
Lays to rest on dusty shelves
Lacked motivation
Now seeks change to shine talents
Life needs an undo button

[Tanka]

Revitalized Passions

Heartbeat of passions
not flatlined, slow beats pulsing
'til revitalized

[Haiku]

Reemerged Hiatus...

Reemerged. Creative hiatus yields revitalized contemplations.

[Six-Word Memoir]

Inspired Return

Taking time to catch one's breath
allows one to return
spirit refreshed
ready to take on the world
where within one's mind
newly inspired notions swirl

[Free Form]

Passion Productivity's Payout

Produce as much of
this passion of mine, even
if unrewarded...

[Haiku]

Profitable Poetry
[Prose]

As strokes of inspiration continue to pour my heart and soul onto paper once more, it's not of any surprise realization that poetry IS my passion.

Poetry SHOULD be my profitable career...
    not just in hopes of a career full of monetary profits, but in wanting need of a career full of endless inspirations that challenge, guide, question all notions of this life we live – a career which allows me to continually flourish in heart, spirit, and mind.

For whenever life throws its curveballs, for better or for worse... you, dear poetry, I forever turn to.

For years I've endlessly...
    profited in the wealth of knowledge you've bestowed upon me, slaving hours on end, sacrificing sleep for gratification of satisfaction sought and found within the walls of your written sanctions, immersing my whole being in pools of poetic thought surfacing from beneath heartfelt emotions.

No more do I wish to humor, in disheartening fashion,
    the notion that I must cloak this wanting need of a career of greater fulfillment, grounded by an unending passion forever taking a backseat, where dreams lay in wait as passengers to more pressing matters at hand... the survival of one's living situations must rest in hands of monetary profits, the driving force that gets us through to the next day, but how many more times must I pull the emergency brake that halts the continuation of a dream I'm forever chasing?

Unwillingly, I find myself searching for... accepting...
jobs of which almost anyone of any skill... can seem to possess.

The truth at hand, the truth that drives my inner core
to swerve and change lanes when possible is...

I desire to be the Waldo of the working world, the one who...
    stands out, noticed by one and all for the unique talent I possess,
    a talent that although similar to some, always remains different
    and unique to me and only me.

Yet, as I continue to join the ranks of the working elite,
    somehow I still manage to blend in,
    becoming less and less the Waldo one finds...
    less and less the one different from the crowd
    because I've followed my own destined path,
    more and more the same as the crowd
    because I've always found it more urgent
    to choose the path of monetary gain over passion
    each time I reach that bypass.

Inherently, I've always known...
    poetry SHOULD be my profitable career!

Profitable in inspirations of written sanctions fascinatingly
flourishing the growth of my heart, spirit, and mind while
providing me the best of both worlds, where I, for once, could
have my cake and eat it too...

Profitable poetry which sustains this life I live monetarily...

Where the value of life living meets the value of passion lived!

At the Kiss of Twilight

"I like the night. Without the dark, we'd never see the stars."

- Stephenie Meyer

Perfection
[Prose]

Perfection
is in the eye of the beholder
lying amidst the realms of imperfections
we see in our reflections
of life seasoned with such uncertainty.

How can one learn
to correct flaws
masked in stress
which keeps one depressed,
where reasoning waits in shadows,
clouded by negative vessels
which rattle the deepest caverns
of our heart and soul?

Learning...
comes from a knowledgeable growth,
within a mind stroked
through divine intervention.

A belief in a higher power
may make some cower
but for those who strive
to overcome flawless imperfections,
by believing in Him,
He who sees a shining light
of perfection in all,
one may come
to finally find perfection
within one's own reflection...

Heart-Cry

Echoing reverberations
Of my pain's suffering ailments
Never ceasing to allow
My heart-cry to be heard
For all that echoes
Loud and clear
Through my silent tears
Is this pain I face...

Pain I can't bear...

Pain that anguishes me...

To the depths of my soul...

Creating an imbalance
Between my heart and mind
Clouding my thoughts
Preying on my emotions
Without any sense of reason
All I can do when trapped
Drowning in such misery

Is...

Just...

RELEASE!

Release all the emotion
Hidden behind my heart-cry
Where all that can be heard
Is my pained affliction

SCREAM!

SHOUT!

MOAN!

Release it all out...

Before I may soon fade out...

Speak Of My Name
[Prose]

Speak of my name,
the only sound which breaks
this deaf voice spoken
in silent cries.

Relinquish me of that
which burdens my inked pages
seeking re-written escapes
from within bound cages.

Speak of my name...
never shall I be called by the name *"LOST"*,
the one who wanders this world aimlessly,
struggling to remain untamed
by the devils of this earth.

Let me be known by the name *"FOUND"*,
for within Him my faith resides;
He is the soldier of the night
pushing me through each storm,
finding my lost destiny for me...

The Promise of a Yes

Life can get discouraging but one thing's for sure,

I will never give up!

A yes answer,

a change for the better,

is somewhere out there

lurking...

Living On A Prayer

On bended knee
Hands clasped tight
Head bent down
Living on a prayer tonight

Whispers of change
Escape my lips
In hopes to reach
Past Heaven's eclipse

Testing my *FAITH*
In *MIRACLES* out of sight
Remaining *HOPEFUL*
I'll see Heaven's *LIGHT*

As day by day
Hope slowly disappears
In my long wait for answers
Have my prayers reached God's ears?

So night after night
With tear-filled eyes
I drop to my knees
Begin my pleading cries

Lord, please hear my *PRAYER*
My *WHISPERS* of change
I *SEEK* a better *LIFE* for me or for others
Can this somehow be *ARRANGED*?

From my lips, to angels, to you
I'll be living on a prayer
Preserving faith and belief in miracles
'Til my prayers receive your answer

Moonlight Magic of Whispered Wishes

Moonlight drapes upon my dream world
in colors galore

Candlelit heavens romanticizing
hopeful intuitions

Swirling refractals of
misguided dreams

Find their way amongst
the rising aurora

The dance of evening wonderments
sparkle like stars

In the shadows lurks wishes
shooting for the moon

Casting light upon hearts mystified
with whispered promises

Impassioned Praise...

Spirits lifted. Faith restored. Impassioned praise.

[Six-Word Memoir]

Unfound Answers...

Questions and wonderments... unfound definitive answers.

[Six-Word Memoir]

Will We Pass God's Test?
[Prose]

Inevitable,
is the possibility of change,
an unending cycle that begins and ends
each time reminding us to never become
too complacent with the life we
live.

Therefore He,
for who our life we give,
pushes us into dire situations unwanted,
in hopes that we remember
Him.

And that by
believing in Him, a higher power,
His challenges have been placed in strategic ways
which put us to the test, this ultimate unending "school-day",
as we seek to graduate, wearing golden vests,
arriving to face, He who grants that ultimate
grade…

One
question forever lingering...
Will we pass life's uncertain test
to get us through that golden gate
of Heaven's Peaceful
Rest?

At The Kiss of Twilight

Lonesome I stand on barren ground
My leaves all fallen, my soul unveiled
Exposed are my insecurities

My beauty disappears into the shadows
As to the break of dawn I seek
Revival of my luscious growth

Through the evening hours
My soul's weary branches sway in the wind
Reaching towards salvation

To touch the tips of Heaven's light
Where uncertain hopes come alive
At the kiss of twilight

Explore Poetic Forms

ACROSTIC (ACRONYM) – Acronyms form a word ("abbreviation") using first letter of each word in a phrase whereas acrostics uses first letter of each line to create a word/message vertically within the poem itself. Does not have to rhyme. Other variations: alphabet order (Abecedarian), in middle (Mesostic), at end (Telestich), both at the front (left) and end (right) to read a phrase/message on both sides of poem (Double Acrostic). ex. p. 75

ANAPHORA – Repetition of words or phrases at beginning of a group of sentences, clauses, or poetic lines. ex. p. 19, 39, 109

CINQUAIN (QUINTET) – A 5-line poem/stanza/verse. Lines can follow a syllabic pattern of 2-4-6-8-2. Can also follow various rhyming patterns such as: ABABB, ABAAB, or ABCCB. ex. pp. 64, 92, 158

COUPLET – Consists of two consecutive lines of verse. Can be rhymed or unrhymed, metered or free verse. ex. pp. 5, 21, 22, 97

HAIKU – A 3-line poem of 17 syllables following syllabic pattern of 5-7-5.
ex. pp. 19, 26, 39, 41, 44, 61, 66, 67, 74, 76, 82, 87, 88, 91, 95, 100, 119, 121, 133, 140, 152, 158, 172, 174, 175

LAI NOUVEAU – Poem with 8-line stanzas using a 5-syllabled couplet followed by a 2-syllable line with rhyming pattern A-A-B-A-A-B-A-A. The first two lines are the refrain alternating as the last lines in subsequent verses with the last verse including both refrain lines in reverse order. ex. p. 79

MESOSTICS – A poem arranging words so that a vertical word/phrase intersects the lines of horizontal text. ex. p. 33, 86

MONOSTICH (ONE SENTENCE POEM) – A single line that constitutes the entire poem in minimal words. ex. p. 100

PANTOUM – Quatrains with second and fourth line repeated in next stanza as first and third line, etc. Last line is often same as the first line. Does not have to rhyme. If rhyming, can follow patterns AABB or ABAB. ex. pp. 105, 125

PROSE – Typically written without line breaks, in paragraph form, using punctuation and poetic devices. ex. pp. 147, 176, 181, 184, 189

QUATRAIN – A 4-line stanza/verse. Does not have to rhyme; rhyming patterns vary: AABB, ABAB, ABBA. ex. p. 17, 40, 52, 62, 63, 84, 93, 96, 122, 126, 134, 157, 159

SESTINA — Consists of 6 stanzas with 6 lines each and followed by a 3-line envoi. The end words of the first stanza lines are repeated in a different order for subsequent stanzas. The envoi contains all six end words, two per line (in the middle and at the end of the three lines). Pattern is as follows: ABCDEF / FAEBDC / CFDABE / ECBFAD / DEACFB / BDFECA / FB / AD / EC
ex. p. 34

SIX-WORD MEMOIR - Telling of a story by only using six words. ex. pp. 4, 9, 12, 16, 19, 20, 26, 40, 41, 48, 61, 66, 67, 74, 75, 83, 88, 91, 95, 107, 108, 115, 121, 1258, 129, 132, 133, 164, 166, 169, 171, 172, 174, 188, 195

TANKA — A poem of 31 syllables across 5 lines with syllabic pattern of 5-7-5-7-7. ex. pp. 36, 124, 174

TRIOLET — An 8-line poem using only two rhymes with a pattern of ABaAabAB. The first line is repeated in the fourth and seventh lines and the second line is also the last line (capital letters indicate repeating lines).
ex. pp. 77, 146

VILLANELLE — A 19-line poem of 5 tercets (3-line stanzas) and a quatrain (4-line stanza) with rhyme scheme (ABA ABA ABA ABA ABA ABAA). First and third lines of opening tercet become alternating repeating refrains as final line of each subsequent tercet and as the two final lines (line 1 = 6, 12, 18 and line 3 = 9, 15, 19). ex. p. 114

Meet Your Poet

Easter Dodds is a romantic at heart and her love of poetry stems from her passion to express herself creatively through the art of the written word. Experiences help shape her crafted words of wisdom about love, relationships, and life's varied experiences.

Writing is most certainly in her genes, for her father's a poet/writer as well! Her extensive collection of poetry found its roots during her high school years and she has continued writing since then.

She's always said, "My poetry's a diary, I share with the world" and she hopes that her poetry has and will continue to find its way into the hearts of many.

With her debut book of poetry, Reach for the Light, she is realizing one of her own dreams as she seeks to help others realize theirs.

Discover more of Easter "Poetik Desire" Dodds' poetry published in...
Printed Editions:
- *INT'L LIBRARY OF POETRY (POETRY.COM):*
  - America at the Millennium: Best Poems and Poets of 20th Century (2000)
  - Poetry's Elite: The Best Poets of 2000 (2001)
- *MAGNAPOETS:* Issue 6 (July 2010)
- *GUERILLA IGNITION:*
  - Only the People Speak These Winds: Volume 1 (2012)
  - Only the People Speak These Winds: Volume 2 (2013)
- *SIX WORD MEMOIRS:*
  - The Best Advice in Six Words (2015)
  - A Terrible, Horrible, No Good Year: Stories on the Pandemic (2021)
- *READ OR GREEN BOOKS:*
  - Touching Tongues: A Women's Erotica Anthology (2021)
  - American Graveyard Vol. 2 Anthology (2025)
- *PGN PUBLISHING:*
  - Season 2 Black and White Anthology (2025)
- *WIDER PERSPECTIVES PUBLISHING:*
  - The Poet's Domain: Vol. 39, As You Like It (2025)

Online Editions:

- ♦ linktr.ee/poetikdesire
- ♦ SixWordMemoirs.com as PoeticPisces
- ♦ Facebook and Instagram as PoetikDesire
- ♦ *ILLOGICAL MUSE:* Fall 2010 Issue (Sept 1st)
- ♦ *POET SPEAK:*
  - Issue 3 (Apr 2011),   Issue 5 (Jul 2011),
  - Issue 8 (Jan 2012),   Issue 9 (Feb 2012),
  - Issue 11 (Apr 2012),   Issue 59 (May 2025)
- ♦ *GUERILLA IGNITION:*
  - Featured on spoken word album: Feminine Anarchy: Vol. 1 (Feb 2015)
- ♦ *MAYARI LITERATURE:*
  - Volume 2, Special Valentine Issue ii (Feb. 2025), Part 2 (Feb 14th), Part 4 (Feb 28th)
  - Volume 2, Issue iii: Trajectory (April 15, 2025)
- ♦ *MOONLIT WEAVER COLLECTIVE:*
  A Journey Under the Moonlight: Anniversary Poetry Anthology Year One (June 2025)
- ♦ *POETIC REVERIES:*
  Issue No.11: Returning to the Sea (August 2025)

linktr.ee/poetikdesire

Life's final draft unscripted 'til death.

[*Six-Word Memoir]

Colophon

Wider Perspectives Publishing regrets to have to announce that the ongoing Colophon page, used to tout artists published in books from WPP, has to be reworked. This is due to the growing library of fine writers coming out of, or even into, the Hampton Roads area of Virginia.

Samantha Casey
Donna Burnett-Robinson
Faith Griffin
Se'Mon-Michelle Rosser
Lisa M. Kendrick
Cassandra IsFree
Nich (Nicholis Williams)
Samantha Geovjian Clarke
Natalie Morison-Uzzle
Gus Woodward II
Patsy Bickerstaff
Edith Blake
Jack Cassada
Dezz
Luana Portales
Daniel Garwood
Jada Hollingsworth
Tabetha Moon House
Travis Hailes- Virgo, thePoet
Nick Marickovich
Grey Hues
Rivers Raye
Madeline Garcia
Chichi Iwuorie
Symay Rhodes
Tanya Cunningham
    (Scientific Eve)
Terra Leigh
Raymond M. Simmons
Samantha Borders-Shoemaker
Taz Weysweete'

Ann Shalaski
Jade Leonard
Darean Polk
Bobby K. (The Poor Man's Poet)
J. Scott Wilson (Teech!)
Charles Wilson
Gloria Darlene Mann
Neil Spirtas
Jorge Mendez & JT Williams
Sarah Eileen Williams
Stephanie Diana (Noftz)
Shanya – Lady S.
Jason Brown (Drk Mtr)
Kailyn Rae Sasso
Crickyt J. Expression

Martina Champion
Crystal Nolen
Catherine TL Hodges
Kent Knowlton
Maria April C.
James Harry Wilson

the Hampton Roads
   Artistic Collective (757
   Perspectives) &
The Poet's Domain
are all WPP literary journals in cooperation with Scientific Eve or Live Wire Press

Check for those artists on FaceBook, Instagram, the Virginia Poetry Online channel on YouTube, and other social media.

www.ingramcontent.com/pod-product-compliance
Lightning Source LLC
Chambersburg PA
CBHW020704270326
41928CB00005B/253